EDWIN MORGAN TWENTIES

MENAGERIE

CELEBRATING EDWIN MORGAN'S
CENTENARY

Love
Scotland
Menagerie
Take Heart
Space and Spaces

EDWIN MORGAN TWENTIES

MENAGERIE

SELECTED POEMS

Introduced by
Michael Rosen

Polygon

in association with
Carcanet

First published in Great Britain in 2020 by
Polygon, an imprint of Birlinn Ltd, in association with
Carcanet Press Ltd

Birlinn Ltd
West Newington House
10 Newington Road
Edinburgh EH9 1QS

9 8 7 6 5 4 3 2 1

www.polygonbooks.co.uk

ISBN 978 1 84697 543 1

British Library Cataloguing-in-Publication Data
A catalogue record for this book is available
from the British Library.

The publisher gratefully acknowledges investment from
Creative Scotland towards the publication of this book.

Typeset in Verdigris MVB by Polygon, Edinburgh
Printed and bound by Gutenberg, Malta

CONTENTS

Introduction   vii

The Bearsden Shark   3
Bees' Nest   5
Clydesdale   6
A Defence   8
from The Glasgow Subway Poems
   The Giraffe   10
   The Piranhas   11
The Dolphin's Song   12
A Good Deed   13
Grendel   15
A Gull   17
Hyena   19
Instamatic Glasgow October 1972   22
The Loch Ness Monster's Song   23
Midge   24
Siesta of a Hungarian Snake   26
The Starlings in George Square   27
The Third Day of the Wolf   31
Trilobites   34
The White Rhinoceros   35
Zoo   37

INTRODUCTION

It was great to discover Edwin Morgan's poems in the 1970s. I'm sure he had discovered himself for a good few years before that (!), but coming from London and not having seen him perform, I can remember my delight at seeing such playful yet thoughtful poetry. At the time I was working with a teacher from Nottingham in producing an anthology based on the spoken word. Our guiding idea was to find poems that had the tenor of the spoken voice, a kind of 'oral poetry on the page' we called it, based on W.H. Auden's expression, 'memorable speech'. When we came across Edwin's poems we knew we had found something that was just right for the job. We performed them to each other, savouring the words, the subtle changes in rhythm and mood. Yes, these would be ideal for children and school students to share, perform, adapt, and make up their own – part of the flow of poetry we were trying to engender.

Since that time, I have heard Edwin on the radio and come across his poems elsewhere. Sadly, I didn't ever see him perform his poems live, but I could hear in his voice on the air, and in lifting the poems off the page myself, the wry humour, gentle moods and occasional melancholy.

It's not easy to sustain poetry by poets who are no longer around to stomp the long miles away from home, perform in unfamiliar rooms and get back home late at night. We have to keep thinking and rethinking of new ways to put their poems in view. This selection of animal poems is a necessary and welcome contribution, and it takes me back to the joy of my first 'discovery' of Edwin's poetry as my friend and I performed his work surrounded by copies of the poems.

Michael Rosen

MENAGERIE

THE BEARSDEN SHARK

O what a whack of a black of a sleek sweet cheeky
   tail in its big blue den
Of water! There were no bears then!
Waterworld it was, warm and salty, wet and scary,
Wild shapes, no ships, no sheep, no sheep-dip, a
   deep deep, very!
Fish but no fishermen, no fishmen, no kingfishers, no kings,
Fish fishing for fish, yes, anglers, rays, jaws, shocks, wings,
And all those early murky milky things,
Stings on strings, things that spring.
Through shoal and shining flock and froth and freath and
   freaky frisky flashers, like a liner,
The Bearsden shark coasts casually, kinglily, killingly
   casual, casing the scales, lazily pacing and chasing, lord
   of the place, of the plaice, lordly diner.
Little does he know of land and ocean, change and chance.
Little would he care if he knew. Little would he change if he
   cared. Little would he love if he changed it. His is
   reality without remorse or romance.
Heroic long-dead creature, waiting in death
To be discovered, uncovered, recovered, recalled from the cold

solid soil that never felt your breath:
We have you in a fosse, a fossil, a fragile long-forgotten
    force of our growing, growling, grounded, founded but
    bounding, bonding and unbonding earth.

Dreams and Other Nightmares
(Mariscat Press, 2010)

BEES' NEST

busybykeobloodybizzinbees
bloodybusybykeobizzinbees
bizzinbloodybykeobusybees
busybloodybykeobizzinbees
bloodybykeobusybizzinbees
bizzinbykeobloodybusybees
busybykeobizzinbloodybees
bloodybykeobizzinbusybees
bizzinbusybykoebloodybees
busybizzinbykeobloodybees
bloodybizzinbykeobusybees
bizzinbusybloodybykeobees

Starryveldt
(Eugen Gomringer Press, 1965)

CLYDESDALE

go
   fetlocksnow
          go
            gullfurrow
                 go

go
   brassglow
          go
            sweatflow
               go

go
   plodknow
          go
            clodshow
               go

go
   leatherbelow
          go
            potatothrow
               go

go
  growfellow

       go
         crowfollow

             go

go
  Balerno

       go
         Palerno

            whoa

The Horseman's Word
(Akros Publications, 1970)

A DEFENCE

I am told I should not love him, the magpie,
that he's a bully, but then I watch them bouncing
along the grass, chattering, black and white and
he and she, twigs in beak, the tree-top swaying
with half a nest in a hail-shower, the magpies
seeing off crows and gulls – a feint of mobbing
but who knows – eyeing a lost swan waddling
down the pavement, off course from Bingham's waters,
the smart bright bold bad pairing caring magpies
whose nest was blown down last December, back now
to build again, to breed again, to bring us
a batch of tumbling clockwork liquorice allsorts,
spruce, spliced, diced, learning to prance and hurtle
through evening and morning sycamores with what must be
something like happiness, the magpies, cocky,
hungry, handsome, an eye-catching flash for that
black and white collie to bark at, and the black and

white cat lurking under the car-bonnet
to lash a bushy tail at, and this page, seeing
these things, first white, now white and black, to pay its
tribute to, and lay out, thus, its pleasure.

Hold Hands among the Atoms
(Mariscat Press, 1991)

from THE GLASGOW SUBWAY POEMS

THE GIRAFFE

The subway giraffe
keeps its head down.
It has a special joint
in its neck. Its mother
is known to have been friendly
with an excavator.
It feeds on old tickets,
a cold chip or two,
makes do with cigarette-ends
but shivers with pleasure
at a scatter of rings
torn off from cans,
smacks its lips
as the metal rattles
down to its stomach.
The neighbours nod wisely:
'Favours his da.'

THE PIRANHAS

Did anyone tell you
that in each subway train
there is one special seat
with a small hole in it
and underneath the seat
is a tank of piranha-fish
which have not been fed
for quite some time.
The fish become agitated
by the shoogling of the train
and jump up through the seat.
The resulting skeletons
of unlucky passengers
turn an honest penny
for the transport executive,
hanging far and wide
in medical schools.

Glasgow Poster Poems
(National Book League
Scotland, 1983)

THE DOLPHIN'S SONG

Man is a fool
as a rule
but we must humour him in school.
So far he only plays with hoops
but we suspect he talks
and every time he looks
at us we blow our tops
and surface laughing – really
we must try to communicate
before it is too late
with the silly
suicidal but engaging skate.

Collected Poems
(Carcanet Press, 1990)

A GOOD DEED

Some say Munchausen is a swashbuckler,
Too ready with knife and gun, too wild of tongue.
Dear friends, it is not for me to defend myself.
I simply lay my life on the line before you.
It is up to you to decide. So what am I?
I was a captain in the Empress of Russia's service.
I have killed some Turks. At the Siege of Gibraltar
I helped the British. I have killed some Spaniards.
But these were wars, where 'Thou shalt not kill'
Invites derision. I have killed some animals,
Many in sport, many in self-defence:
Is that bad? I think we need a referendum!

But speaking of animals: I give you a story.
I was out hunting one summer day
Deep in the forests of Lithuania
When I saw in the distance two wild pigs
Walking in line. I shot at them, but missed,
Or almost missed. The one in front ran off,
Seemingly unharmed, but letting out a yelp.
The other one stood still – extraordinary –
Waiting patiently till I came up to her,

An old sow with her head down, silent.
I passed a hand in front of her; she was blind.
Her jaws still held a fragment of the tail
Her son had led her with. She stood helpless,
Afraid to move, yet not afraid of me,
Smell of man and smoking gun: I think
She sensed I was not now the enemy.
I grasped the piece of tail my shot had left
And led the creature, trotting docile behind me,
Back to her den.
          Who are the cynics then?
I invented the story to appear in a better light?
Did I, would I, could I help the poor beast?
I know the answer. I'm sure you do too.

Tales from Baron Munchausen
(Mariscat Press, 2005)

GRENDEL

It is being nearly human
gives me this spectacular darkness.
The light does not know what to do with me.
I rise like mist and I go down like water.
I saw them soused with wine behind their windows.
I watched them making love, twisting like snakes.
I heard a blind man pick the strings, and sing.
There are torches everywhere, there are faces
swimming in shine and sweat and beer and grins and greed.
There are tapers confusing the stacked spears.
There are queens on their knees at idols, crosses, lamps.
There are handstand clowns knocked headlong by maudlin
    heroes.
There are candles in the sleazy bowers, the whores
sleep all day with mice across their feet.
The slung warhorn gleams in the drizzle,
the horses shift their hooves and shiver.
It is all a pestilence, life within life
and movement within movement, lips meeting,
grooming of mares, roofs plated with gold,
hunted pelts laid on kings,
neck-veins bursting from greasy torques,
pouches of coins gamed off, slaves and outlaws
eating hailstones under heaven.

Who would be a man? Who would be the winter sparrow
that flies at night by mistake into a lighted hall
and flutters the length of it in zigzag panic,
dazed and terrified by the heat and noise and smoke,
the drink-fumes and the oaths, the guttering flames,
feast-bones thrown to a snarl of wolfhounds,
flash of swords in sodden sorry quarrels,
till at last he sees the other door
and skims out in relief and joy
into the stormy dark?
– Black grove, black lake, black sky,
no shoe or keel or wing undoes your stillness
as I plod through the fens and prowl
in my own place and sometimes stand many hours, as now,
above those unreflecting waters, reflecting as I can
on men, and on their hideous clamorous brilliance
that beats the ravens' beaks into the ground
and douses a million funeral pyres.

Poems of Thirty Years
(Carcanet Press, 1983)

A GULL

A seagull stood on my window-ledge today,
said nothing, but had a good look inside.
That was a cold inspection I can tell you!
North winds, icebergs, flash of salt
crashed through the glass without a sound.
He shifted from leg to leg, swivelled his head.
There was not a fish in the house – only me.
Did he smell my flesh, that white one? Did he think
I would soon open the window and scatter bread?
Calculation in those eyes is quick.
'I tell you, my chick, there is food *everywhere*.'
He eyed my furniture, my plants, an apple.
Perhaps he was a mutation, a supergull.
Perhaps he was, instead, a visitation
which only used that tight firm forward body
to bring the waste and dread of open waters,
foundered voyages, matchless predators,
into a dry room. I knew nothing.
I moved; I moved an arm. When the thing saw

the shadow of that, it suddenly flapped,
scuttered claws along the sill, and was off,
silent still. Who would be next for those eyes,
I wondered, and were they ready, and in order?

Cathures: New Poems 1997–2001
(Carcanet Press/Mariscat Press, 2002)

HYENA

I am waiting for you.
I have been travelling all morning through the bush
and not eaten.
I am lying at the edge of the bush
on a dusty path that leads from the burnt-out kraal.
I am panting, it is midday, I found no water-hole.
I am very fierce without food and although my eyes
are screwed to slits against the sun
you must believe I am prepared to spring.

What do you think of me?
I have a rough coat like Africa.
I am crafty with dark spots
like the bush-tufted plains of Africa.
I sprawl as a shaggy bundle of gathered energy
like Africa sprawling in its waters.
I trot, I lope, I slaver, I am a ranger.
I hunch my shoulders. I eat the dead.

Do you like my song?
When the moon pours hard and cold on the veldt
I sing, and I am the slave of darkness.
Over the stone walls and the mud walls and the ruined places

and the owls, the moonlight falls.
I sniff a broken drum. I bristle. My pelt is silver.
I howl my song to the moon – up it goes.
Would you meet me there in the waste places?

It is said I am a good match
for a dead lion. I put my muzzle
at his golden flanks, and tear. He
is my golden supper, but my tastes are easy.
I have a crowd of fangs, and I use them.
Oh and my tongue – do you like me
when it comes lolling out over my jaw
very long, and I am laughing?
I am not laughing.
But I am not snarling either, only
panting in the sun, showing you
what I grip
carrion with.

I am waiting
for the foot to slide,
for the heart to seize,
for the leaping sinews to go slack,
for the fight to the death to be fought to the death,
for a glazing eye and the rumour of blood.
I am crouching in my dry shadows
till you are ready for me.
My place is to pick you clean
and leave your bones to the wind.

From Glasgow to Saturn

(Carcanet Press, 1973)

INSTAMATIC GLASGOW OCTOBER 1972

At the Old Ship Bank pub in Saltmarket
a milk-lapping contest is in progress.
A dozen very assorted Bridgeton cats
have sprung from their starting-blocks
to get their heads down in the gleaming saucers.
In the middle of the picture
young Tiny is about to win his bottle of whisky
by kittening through the sweet half-gill
in one minute forty seconds flat, but
Sarah, at the end of the line,
self-contained and silver-grey,
has sat down with her back to the saucer
and surveys the photographers calmly.
She is a cat who does not like milk.

Grafts/Takes
(Mariscat Press, 1983)

THE LOCH NESS MONSTER'S SONG

Sssnnnwhuffffll?
Hnwhuffl hhnnwfl hnfl hfl?
Gdroblboblhobngbl gbl gl g g g g glbgl.
Drublhaflablhaflubhafgabhaflhafl fl fl –
gm grawwwww grf grawf awfgm graw gm.
Hovoplodok-doplodovok-plovodokot-doplodokosh?
Splgraw fok fok splgrafhatchgabrlgabrl fok splfok!
Zgra kra gka fok!
Grof grawff gahf?
Gombl mbl bl –
blm plm,
blm plm,
blm plm,
blp.

Twelve Songs

(The Castlelaw Press, 1970)

MIDGE

The evening is perfect, my sisters.
The loch lies silent, the air is still.
The sun's last rays linger over the water
and there is a faint smirr, almost a smudge
of summer rain. Sisters, I smell supper,
and what is more perfect than supper?
It is emerging from the wood,
in twos and threes, a dozen in all,
making such a chatter and a clatter
as it reaches the rocky shore,
admiring the arrangements of the light.
See the innocents, my sisters,
the clumsy ones, the laughing ones,
the rolled-up sleeves and the flapping shorts,
there is even a kilt (god of the midges,
you are good to us!) So gather your forces,
leave your tree-trunks, forsake the rushes,
fly up from the sour brown mosses
to the sweet flesh of face and forearm.
Think of your eggs. What does the egg need?
Blood, and blood. Blood is what the egg needs.
Our men have done their bit, they've gone,

it was all they were good for, poor dears. Now
it is up to us. The egg is quietly screaming
for supper, blood, supper, blood, supper!
Attack, my little Draculas, my Amazons!
Look at those flailing arms and stamping feet.
They're running, swatting, swearing, oh they're hopeless.
Keep at them, ladies. This is a feast.
This is a midsummer night's dream.
Soon we shall all lie down filled and rich,
and lay, and lay, and lay, and lay, and lay.

Virtual and Other Realities
(Carcanet Press, 1997)

SIESTA OF A HUNGARIAN SNAKE

s sz sz SZ sz SZ sz ZS zs ZS zs zs z

The Second Life
(Edinburgh University Press, 1968)

THE STARLINGS IN GEORGE SQUARE

I

Sundown on the high stonefields!
The darkening roofscape stirs –
thick – alive with starlings
gathered singing in the square –
like a shower of arrows they cross
the flash of a western window,
they bead the wires with jet,
they nestle preening by the lamps
and shine, sidling by the lamps
and sing, shining, they stir
the homeward hurrying crowds.
A man looks up and points
smiling to his son beside him
wide-eyed at the clamour on those cliffs –
it sinks, shrills out in waves,
levels to a happy murmur,
scatters in swooping arcs,
a stab of confused sweetness
that pierces the boy like a story,
a story more than a song.
He will never forget that evening,
the silhouette of the roofs,
the starlings by the lamps.

The City Chambers are hopping mad.
Councillors with rubber plugs in their ears!
Secretaries closing windows!
Window-cleaners want protection and danger money.
The Lord Provost can't hear herself think, man.
What's that?
Lord Provost, can't hear herself think.

At the General Post Office
the clerk writes Three Pounds Starling in the savings-books.
Each telephone-booth is like an aviary.
I tried to send a parcel to County Kerry but –
The cables to Cairo got fankled, sir.
What's that?
I said the cables to Cairo got fankled.

And as for the City Information Bureau –
I'm sorry I can't quite chirrup did you twit –
No I wanted to twee but perhaps you can't cheep –
Would you try once again, that's better, I – sweet –
When's the last boat to Milngavie? Tweet?
What's that?
I said when's the last boat to Milngavie?

III

There is nothing for it now but scaffolding:
clamp it together, send for the bird-men,
Scarecrow Strip for the window-ledge landings,
Cameron's Repellent on the overhead wires.
Armour our pediments against eavesdroppers.
This is a human outpost. Save our statues.
Send back the jungle. And think of the joke:
as it says in the papers, It is very comical
to watch them alight on the plastic rollers
and take a tumble. So it doesn't kill them?
All right, so who's complaining? This isn't Peking
where they shoot the sparrows for hygiene and cash.
We're all humanitarians, locked in our cliff-dwellings
encased in our repellent, guano-free and guilt-free.
The Lord Provost sings in her marble hacienda.
The Postmaster-General licks an audible stamp.
Sir Walter is vexed that his column's deserted.
I wonder if we really deserve starlings?
There is something to be said for these joyous messengers
that we repel in our indignant orderliness.
They lift up the eyes, they lighten the heart,
and some day we'll decipher that sweet frenzied whistling

as they wheel and settle along our hard roofs
and take those grey buttresses for home.
One thing we know they say, after their fashion.
They like the warm cliffs of man.

The Second Life
(Edinburgh University Press, 1968)

THE THIRD DAY OF THE WOLF

Lock the gates and man the fences!
The lone Canadian timber-wolf
has escaped into the thickets, the ditches, the distances!
Blow the silver whistles!
The zoo-born sniffs the field mist,
the hedgerow leaves, liberty wind
of a cold February Friday.

Saturday trudging, loping, hungry, free but hunted,
dogs tracking, baying, losing scent, shouts dying,
fields dangerous, hills worse, night welcome, but the hunger
now! And Sunday many miles, risking farms, seen panting,
dodging the droning helicopter shadows,
flashing past gardens, wilder, padding along a highway,
twilight, sleepy birdsong, dark safety – till a car
catches the grey thing in its rushing headlights,
throws it to the verge, stunned, ruptured, living, lying,
fangs dimly scrabbling the roots of Hertfordshire.
The haze lifting, the head rising, the legs limping, the run
beginning again, with torches, whispers, smell of men and guns,
far off warning, nearer, receding, wavering, waiting
for a whimper, a twig crack, a blood spot, finding them
and coming on, coming nearer to the starving meeting-place.
Breaking cover as had to be, on the icy morning of Monday,

Monday suddenly opening all its mouths, gulping
with fury at the weary fragment, farmers, keepers, police,
two planes diving again and again to drive it
in terror towards the guns, and the farmer's pet collie
cornering it at last with the understrapper's yap.
The empty belly and mad yellow eyes
waiting for man were then shot,
not killed, then bludgeoned,
not killed, then shot,
and killed.

How strong man is
with his helicopters and his planes,
his radios and rifles!
What a god for a collie!
O wild things, wild things
take care, beware of him.
Man mends his fences.
Take care, take strength.
Take care of the warrant
for death. How good
he is at that,
with his dirty sack
ready to lay on you:

it is necessary.
But I have a warrant
to lay this too,
a wreath for wildness,
timber-wolf, timber-wolf.

The Second Life
(Edinburgh University Press, 1968)

TRILOBITES

A grey-blue slab, fanned like a pigeon's wing,
stands on my record cabinet
between a lamp and a speaker.
Trapped in a sea of solid stone
the trilobites still almost swim;
the darker grey of their backs,
thumbnail-sized and thumbnail-shaped,
gives out a dull shine as I switch on the lamp.
I have eight of them; half are crushed, but
two are almost perfect, lacking nothing but the antennas.
My fingertip, coarse and loutish
tracing the three delicate rows of furrowed plates,
tries to read that paleozoic braille
as vainly as the blast of Wagner at their ear
searches for entrance five hundred million years
and a world of air too late. But I would not trade
my family torn by chance from time
for Grecian urn or gold Byzantium.

Collected Poems
(Carcanet Press, 1990)

THE WHITE RHINOCEROS

'Rare over most of its former range'
Webster's Third New International Dictionary

The white rhinoceros was eating phosphorous!
I came up and I shouted Oh no! No! No! –
you'll be extinct in two years! But he shook his ears
and went on snorting, knee-deep in pawpaws,
trundling his hunger, shrugged off the tick-birds,
rolled up his sleeves, kicked over an anthill,
crunched, munched, wonderful windfall,
empty dish. And gored that old beat-up tin tray
for more, it stuck on his horn,
looked up with weird crown on his horn
like a bear with a beehive, began to glow –
as leerie lair bear glows honeybrown –
but he glowed

        white and

            bright and
the safety-catches started to click in the thickets
for more. Run, holy hide – take up your armour –
Run – white horn, tin clown, crown of rain-woods,
venerable shiner! Run, run, run!

And thunders glowing like a phantom
through the bush, beating the guns
this time, but will he always
when his only camouflage
is a world of white?

Save the vulnerable shiners.
Watch the phosphorous trappers.
Smash the poisonous dish.

The Second Life
(Edinburgh University Press, 1968)

ZOO

humpback / haversack / Heidsieck / ho
catamount / catmint / catapult / cahootchy
muntjac / milletcake / mandrake / mowwow
jaguar / jamjar / jauntingcar / jahossa
bullfinch / bandersnatch / backfisch / bawbaw
crocodile / catcall / camomile / cacassophat
starling / sitarstring / skirling / swee
albatross / Anschluss / asterisks / apollapump
chipmunk / Chiang Kai-shek / champak / chouf
bowerbird / Bluebeard / baffleboard / b'hubblybaw
dingo / dustblow / doggo / dump
octopus / office / orifice / oiwa
slowworm / sittingroom / solemn / slinch
hippogriff / halfoff / hurdlescuff / hupcake
vampire / visitor / visor / voo

Dreams and Other Nightmares
(Mariscat Press, 2010)

ABOUT THE AUTHOR

EDWIN MORGAN (1920–2010) was born in Glasgow, and spent his life there except for his six years with the Royal Army Medical Corps in the Middle East. He studied English Literature at the University of Glasgow, where he went on to teach, retiring as Professor Emeritus in 1980. He was appointed Glasgow's Poet Laureate in 1999, and awarded the Queen's Gold Medal for Poetry in 2000. In 2004 he was appointed the first Scots Makar of modern times, and wrote the poem 'For the Opening of the Scottish Parliament' in the same year. His poetry is praised for its linguistic inventiveness, social realism and humane curiosity. He wrote concrete and visual poetry, opera libretti and collaborated with jazz saxophonist Tommy Smith to set his work to music; he was also a translator, playwright and critic. Morgan's work is renowned for its outward-looking internationalism, his poetic gaze moving from Europe to the wider world and into space, yet always returning to Glasgow, whose people and landscape he so memorably evoked and imagined.